the telephone

or L'AMOUR À TROIS

opera
buffa
in
one
act

words and music by
GIAN-CARLO MENOTTI

French Version by
LEON KOCHNITZKY

VOCAL SCORE

Ed. 1910

1993 Printing

G. SCHIRMER, Inc.

DISTRIBUTED BY
HAL•LEONARD®
CORPORATION
7777 W. BLUEMOUND RD. P.O. BOX 13819 MILWAUKEE, WI 53213

T0059100

Characters

•

LUCY
(Soprano)

•

BEN
(Baritone)

The scene is Lucy's apartment

The Telephone was originally written for production by the Ballet Society, and was first presented by that organization with Mr. Menotti's *The Medium* at the Heckscher Theater, New York City, February 18 to 20, 1947. In these performances Marilyn Cotlow took the part of Lucy, and Paul Kwartin appeared as Ben. Leon Barzin conducted two of the performances, Emanuel Balaban the other, while Horace Armistead designed the costumes and scenery.

The Broadway production, based on the Ballet Society's, and presented by Chandler Cowles and Efrem Zimbalist Jr. in association with Edith Lutyens, began at the Ethel Barrymore Theater, May 1, 1947. Frank Rogier took the part of Ben, Miss Cotlow that of Lucy, and Mr. Balaban was the conductor.

Orchestra materials and an arrangement of the orchestral score for two pianos are available on rental.

Instrumentation

Flute
Oboe
Clarinet in B♭
Bassoon
Horn in F
Trumpet in C
Percussion (one player):
    Snare Drum, Bass Drum, Cymbal, Triangle
Piano
Strings

The Telephone

or

L'Amour à Trois

French version by
Léon Kochnitzky

Words and Music by
Gian Carlo Menotti

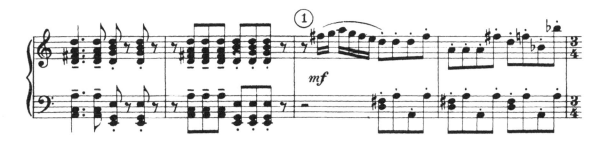

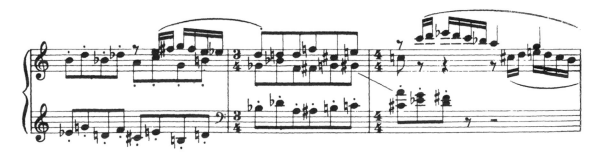

4 Andantino

Allegro vivace

pp

sf

sff

attacca

6

Lucy: Yes, dear? / Oui, cher?

Ben: You know how much I've always liked you... / Vous sa-vez bien que je vous trouve... Well, then... I was just / char-mante.. je vou-lais sa-

Poco meno

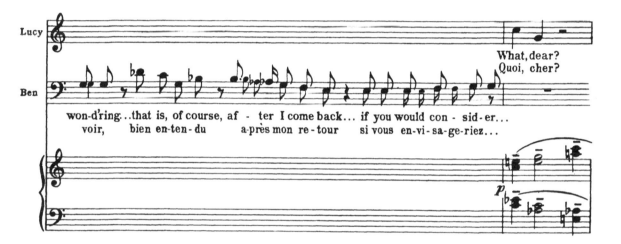

Ben: won-d'ring...that is, of course, af - ter I come back... if you would con - sid-er... / voir, bien en-ten-du a-près mon re-tour si vous en-vi-sa-ge-riez...

Lucy: What, dear? / Quoi, cher?

(the telephone rings)
(sonnerie du téléphone)

Allegro

Lucy: Ex - cuse me. Hel- / Vous per-met - tez? Al -

Ben: I don't quite know how to tell you. / Je ne sais comment vous di - re.

l.h.

8

Lucy

lo! Hel-lo? Oh, Mar - ga-ret, it's you. I am so glad you called, I was just
lo? Al - lo? O Mar - ga-ret, c'est toi comme c'est gen - til vrai-ment et quel plai-

Lucy

think - ing of you. It's been a long time since you called me.
sir d'en-tendre en - fin ta voix, a - près des siècles. __

Lucy

Who? I? I can-not come to - night. No, my dear, I'm not
Qui? Moi? Ce soir c'est im - pos-sible. Non, ma chère, je ne

Lucy

feel - ing ver - y well. When? Where? I wish I could be there!
me sens pas très bien. Quand? Où? Comme je vou-drais y être!

poco rit.   a tempo

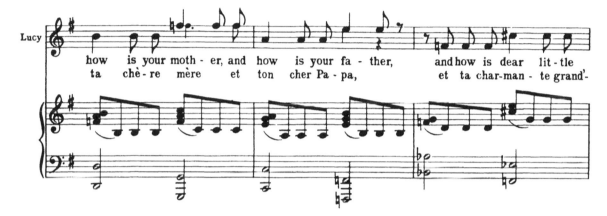

12

41735

14

41735

41735

Andantino

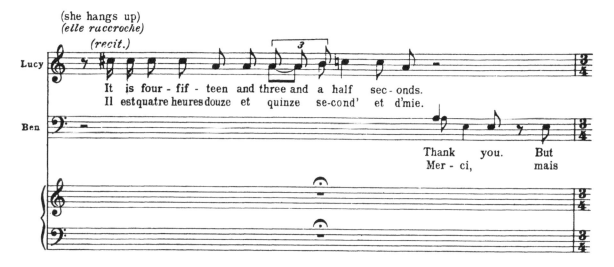

(she hangs up)
(elle raccroche)

(recit.)

Lucy: It is four - fif - teen and three and a half sec - onds.
Il est quatre heures douze et quinze se-cond' et d'mie.

Ben: Thank you. But
Mer - ci, mais

Allegro

Lucy: Of course, what else have I done?
Je vous é - cou - te, mon cher!

Ben: now, please, will you lis-ten to me?
en - fin, vou-lez vous m'en-ten-dre?

Allegro

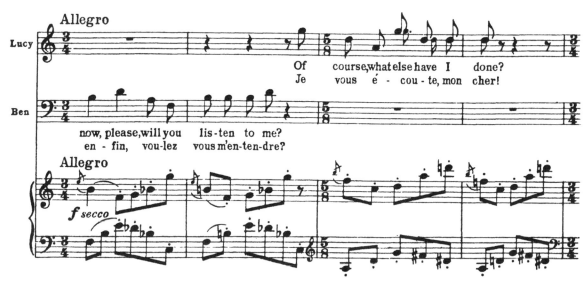

f secco

How dare_____ you say such a thing! Stop us-ing such
Quelle au-dace_____ de me par-ler ain-si! Quelle im-per-ti-

lan-guage! No... yes... no, no, I mean... I swear it is-n't
nen-ce! Non... oui... non, je veux dire... je jure que c'n'est pas

true! How can you be-lieve that I'd say such a
vrai! Com-ment pou-vez-vous croi-re que j'ai dit

thing? Now lis-ten to me! I'm not going to stand it if you call me
ça? As-sez de gros mots, je ne vais pas to-lé-rer ça plus long-

24

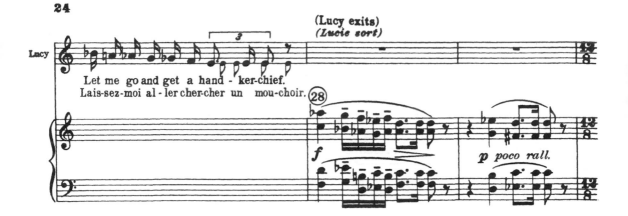

(Lucy exits)
(Lucie sort)

Let me go and get a hand-ker-chief.
Lais-sez-moi al-ler cher-cher un mou-choir.

Andante

Try a-gain and a - gain. What else can a man do ex-cept wait and then
Que peut faire un pauvre homme, es-pé-rer et at-tendre et en-core et en-

try and wait and then try once a - gain? I'd rath-er con-tend with lov-er, hus-band, or
core, en-core es-pé-rer et at - tendre. Il vaut mieux bra - ver u - ne mère, un a-

in - laws, than this two - head - ed mon-ster who comes un-asked and de-vours my
mant que ce monstre à deux têtes qui s'a-mène tou-jours au mau-vais mo-

41735

day. For this thing can't be chal-lenged, can't be poi-soned or
ment. Mais com-ment le com-bat-tre par le fer, le poi-

drowned. It has hun-dreds of lives and miles of um-bil-i-cal cord.
son, quand il a un in-ter-mi-na-ble cor-don om-bi-li-cal.

(He notices a pair of scissors on a table. He arms himself with them and approaches the
(Il aperçoit sur la table une grande paire de ciseaux. Armé des ciseaux il s'approche du

telephone slowly and menacingly)
téléphone avec lenteur et d'un air menaçant)

41735

(Suddenly the telephone rings out loudly and
desperately, like a child crying for help)
*(A ce moment le téléphone se met à sonner
très fort, à coups répétés, comme un petit
enfant qui appelle au secours)*

(Lucy rushes in and takes the telephone protectingly in her arms)
(Lucie rentre en courant, et saisit le téléphone dans ses bras pour le protéger)

Andante moderato

41735

30

Lucy: Jean and I went skat - ing. We got on the trol-ley and met Meg and Mol - ly,
lais au pa - ti - na - ge quand sur le tram-way où j'é-tais a - vec Jeanne j'ai

Lucy: so we sat down next to them. I've known both Meg and Mol-ly for years, and
ren-con-tré Mol - ly et Meg. Ell' sont, je le croyais mes a-mies de -

Lucy: thought they were my friends. ___ But what they have done to me now I'll
puis bien des an - né - es. Mais le coup qu'ell' vienn' de me faire je

Lucy: nev - er, nev - er for - get. ___ They start - ed
ne l'ou-blie-rai ja - mais. ___ Ell' zont vou -

41735

41735

Ben
must tell her I love her, but that thing will not let me, and
dois lui dire que je l'ai - me ce mon - stre ne veut pas. _____ Il

Ben
now I have to go and she will nev - er, and she will nev - er
faut que je m'en aille ell' ne sau - ra ja - mais, ne sau - ra ja -

molto rit.

Lucy
Of course, I said, "Oh, George, my dar - ling, how
Bien sûr, j'ai dit: "O mon p'tit Geor - ges, com -

Ben
know.
mais

molto rit.

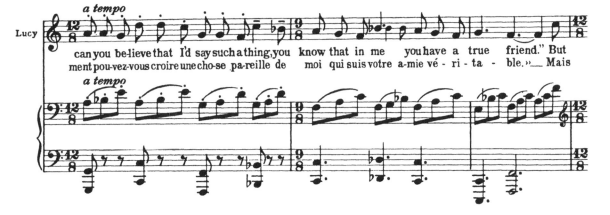

can you be-lieve that I'd say such a thing, you know that in me you have a true friend." But
ment pou-vez-vous croire une cho-se pa-reille de moi qui suis votre a-mie vé - ri - ta - ble.»__ Mais

he would-n't be-lieve me, and cursed __ me up and down, __ and
lui ne m'a pas cru - e mal - gré __ tout c'que j'ai dit, __ il

kept call-ing me names, yes, all sorts of names. __ And then I
m'a dit des in - sul - tes, oui, des in - sul - tes! A - lors j'ai

said, "Oh, George, my dar-ling, if you don't be-lieve me you can call up Phyl-lis and
dit: "O mon p'tit Geor-ges, si vous ne vou-lez pas me croire, a-lors té - lé - pho-

41735

ask her to tell you wheth-er or not it is true."___ Of
nez à Ger-maine et de-man-dez lui si c'est vrai!»___ Bien

course I had to lie,___ what else was I to do?___ But
sûr j'ai du men-tir,___ com-ment faire au-tre chose.___ Mais

oh,___ you'll nev-er know how much I went through. Oh,
oh,___ tu n'sau-ras pas par quoi j'ai pas-sé. Oh,

Oh,___ you'll nev-er know how much I went through.
Oh,___ tu n'sau-ras pas par quoi j'ai pas-sé.

I've
J'at -

38

41735

(At one side of the stage a curtain is drawn, revealing a public telephone booth
somewhere in the city. Ben is seen in it, dialing a number)
(Sur l'un des côtés de la scène, un rideau se lève, découvrant au public une cabine
téléphonique de la ville, où Ben est en train de composer un numéro)

41735

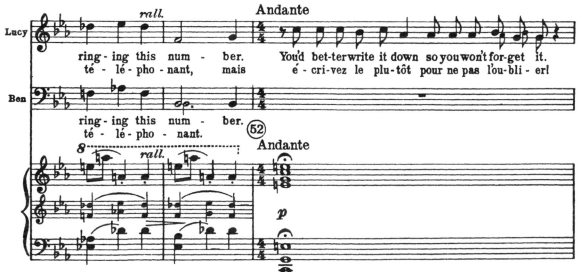

(Ben struggles with a pencil and paper)
(Ben agite un crayon et un carnet)